Round and round

The wheels on my car go round and round.

The wheel on a wheelbarrow goes round and round.

The wheels on a bike go round and round.

The wheels on a pushchair go round and round.

The wheels on a tractor go round and round.

The wheels on a car go round and round.

The wheels on a truck
go round and round.

The wheels on a train go round and round.